A Little English Cookbook

Rosa Mashiter

ILLUSTRATED BY JAN HILL

First published in 1989 by
The Appletree Press Ltd, 19-21 Alfred Street,
Belfast BT2 8DL. *Tel* +44 232 243074
Fax +44 232 246756. Text ©
Rosa Mashiter, 1989. Illustrations ©
Jan Hill, 1989. Printed in the E.C.

British Library Cataloguing in Publication
Data
Mashiter, Rosa
A little English cookbook.
1, Food, English dishes, Recipes
I. Title
641.5942

ISBN 0-86281-217-8

9 8 7 6 5 4 3

Introduction

We are so fortunate in England's green and pleasant land to have such an abundance of fresh seasonal ingredients, and this is reflected in the cooking throughout the breadth of the country. Spring brings us delicious English lamb. Summertime is the time for soft fruits, raspberries, strawberries, black, white and redcurrants, a wealth of salad ingredients, and freshly caught salmon. At the first whiff of autumn, and the first frost, the weekly vegetable market offers a startling array of fresh vegetables, the first game appears in the butcher's window, and good use is made of the cheaper cuts of meat to start producing warming nourishing meals. Winter, and Christmas brings fresh plump turkeys, tight bright green brussel sprouts, and the wonderful aroma of fresh baking wafting from the kitchen. Wherever you go in England you will have the opportunity to discover and enjoy a veritable wealth of good food, a true taste of England.

A note on measures
Imperial, metric and American measures have been used in this book. Use one set of measures only. Where no American measure has been used, as in the case of meat weights, please use the metric measure. All spoon measurements are level rather than heaped. Recipes are for four unless otherwise stated.

Traditional English Breakfast

In 1861 Mrs Beeton said that 'to begin the day well is a grand thing, and a good breakfast at a reasonable hour is an excellent foundation for a day's work, or even a pleasure'. A traditional English breakfast *is* a pleasure, and one that should be savoured, not rushed.

Start with a glass of freshly squeezed orange juice, followed by a bowl of cornflakes lightly sprinkled with sugar, or perhaps with some fresh fruit added.

Some crisply grilled bacon, a sausage or two beautifully browned, accompanied by either a fried or scrambled egg. To scramble eggs, beat two eggs in a bowl and season with salt and pepper. Melt a little butter in a small non-stick saucepan and when the butter starts to foam pour in the beaten egg, and immediately start to stir with a wooden spoon. Remove from the heat as soon as the egg starts to set. Scrambled egg should be runny (if set it will taste quite rubbery).

Grilled tomatoes, sauteed mushrooms, and fried bread (slices of bread fried to a golden brown in lard) are the traditional accompaniments.

To round off breakfast serve tea or coffee, with a rack of freshly made toast, butter and marmalade.

Love Apple Soup

When tomatoes were first found growing as weeds in the maize fields of the Andes they were thought to be poisonous. When they were first introduced to England some two hundred or so years ago it was discovered that they were in fact not poisonous but were thought instead to be a powerful aphrodisiac, and they have never lost their popularity since!

1 lb/450 g firm ripe tomatoes	½ tsp dried basil
	½ tsp dried thyme
1 medium onion	salt and freshly ground black pepper
1 oz/25 g/2 tbsp butter	
	1 tsp sugar
1½ pts/750 ml/3¾ cups chicken stock	small bunch of chives or spring onion tops

Put the tomatoes into a large bowl, cover with boiling water, let stand for one minute then slide off the skins. Chop the tomatoes. Peel and finely chop the onion.

Melt the butter in a saucepan and gently cook the onion over a low heat until soft and transparent, but not browned. Add the tomatoes, stock, herbs and sugar, and season with salt and freshly ground black pepper. Bring to the boil, then lower the heat and let simmer for 15-20 minutes.

Pour into warmed soup bowls, and garnish with a generous sprinkling of finely chopped chives or spring onion tops.

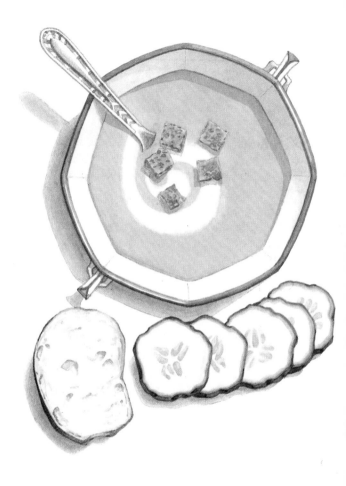

Chilled Cucumber Soup

Introduced from India in the sixteenth century, cucumbers were, and still are, popular as a salad ingredient. Mrs Beeton always maintained that cucumber was a cold food, and I would have to agree and say that they make a delicious summertime soup.

2 cucumbers	1/4 tsp ground cloves
1/2 pt/300 ml/1 1/4 cups water	1 bouquet garni
1 oz/25 g/2 tbsp butter	5 fl oz/150 ml/10 tbsp sour cream
1 small onion	1 tbsp lemon juice
1 tbsp flour	salt and white pepper
1 pt/600 ml/2 1/2 cups chicken stock	chopped fresh mint

Peel and slice the cucumber. Peel and finely chop the onion. Put the cucumber and water into a saucepan and cook until tender. Purée the cucumber and cooking liquid in a food processor or liquidizer.

In a large suacepan melt the butter and fry the onion very gently until soft and transparent. Stir in the flour and mix well. Over a medium heat gradually add the stock, stirring all the time, until the mixture thickens. Bring to the boil and add the cucumber purée, cloves, bouquet garni and lemon juice. Season with salt and pepper. Bring to the boil. Remove from the heat and strain through a sieve. Leave to cool thoroughly, then stir in the sour cream. Chill well before serving in chilled bowls, garnishing the soup with a fine sprinkling of chopped fresh mint.

Farmhouse Vegetable Soup

The English housewife is indeed fortunate to have a wealth of fresh vegetables available all year round. A good West Country farmhouse lunch would consist of a hearty soup accompanied by some fresh crusty bread, perhaps followed by cheese.

2 large onions	*2 pts home-made stock*
1 small cauliflower	*¼ pt/150 ml/½ cup*
2 medium carrots	*natural yoghurt*
3 sticks celery	*salt and freshly ground*
1½ oz/40 g/3 tbsp butter	*pepper*

Peel and finely chop the carrot and onion, chop the celery and break the cauliflower into florettes.

Heat the butter in a heavy-bottomed saucepan, add the vegetables, and cook over a low heat until the vegetables start to soften. Add the stock, season with salt and freshly ground black pepper and simmer until the vegetables are soft. Strain the vegetables, reserving the liquid. Liquidize the vegetables and return to a clean saucepan together with the cooking liquid. Check for seasoning and stir in the yoghurt. Reheat gently – do not boil.

Morecambe Bay Potted Shrimps

To my mind the shrimps of Morecambe Bay are the sweetest and most delicious of all shrimps to be found in England. Eaten simply with a wedge of lemon and some lightly buttered brown bread they are a 'poem', to be savoured, enjoyed and remembered.

---

8 oz/250 g/1 cup butter
1 lb/450 g/2 cups fresh peeled shrimps
blade of mace
pinch of cayenne pepper
pinch of ground nutmeg

Put the butter in a saucepan over a low heat and allow to melt, without browning. Remove from the heat and allow to stand until the sediment sinks to the bottom. Strain through muslin.

Reheat about three-quarters of the butter and stir in the seasonings, followed by the shrimps, over a very low heat until the butter has been absorbed into the shrimps.

Divide into little ramekin dishes or pots, pressing down lightly, and allow to cool completely. Pour over the remaining butter to seal the pots. Chill well before serving.

Devilled Whitebait

Whitebait are delicious tiny little fish, the small fry and sprats. They are caught in great quantities in East Anglia where at Southend an annual Whitebait Festival still takes place celebrating the first catch.

1 lb/450 g whitebait	freshly ground black
4 tbsp flour	pepper
2 tsp curry powder	lemon wedges
½ tsp chilli powder	deep oil for frying

Wash and dry the whitebait on kitchen paper. Put the flour, curry powder, chilli powder and some freshly ground black pepper into a bowl and mix well.

Heat the deep oil. Coat the whitebait (not too many at a time) in the seasoned flour and fry until crisp – it will only take 2-3 minutes, then remove with a slotted spoon and drain on crumpled kitchen paper.

Transfer to a warm serving dish and keep hot in the oven while you cook the rest of the whitebait in batches.

To serve, pile into a linen napkin on a serving plate, garnish with thick lemon wedges and accompany with thinly sliced, buttered brown bread.

Aylesbury Duckling

Now something of a rarity, Aylesbury Duckling is particularly delicious served with an orange sauce.

---

2 duckling
3 large oranges   salt and pepper
Sauce
grated rind and juice of 2 oranges
¾ pt/450 ml/2 cups stock   2 tsp cornflour

Peel and depith the large oranges, divide into quarters and stuff into the body cavities of the ducklings, closing with toothpicks.

Place on a rack in a roasting tin and cook for 30 minutes at gas mark 5, 375°F, 190°C. Remove from the oven, carefully prick the skin all over and return to the oven for a further 30 minutes, or until the juices run clear when a skewer is plunged into the thickest part of the leg.

Remove the duck from the oven and scoop out the oranges and discard. Strain the fat from the roasting tin and add the stock and orange rind. Bring to the boil, lower heat and simmer.

Blend the cornflour with the orange juice and pour into the pan. Cook over a gentle heat until the sauce has thickened and cleared. Brush a little sauce over the breasts of the ducklings and garnish with slices of fresh orange. Serve the sauce separately.

Roast Pheasant

From October to the end of January pheasant is in season in England. Shooting is no longer the prerogative of the rich: nowadays it is possible to buy into a shooting syndicate. Game is much more readily available in the shops and in mid-season it can be quite reasonable in price, although it is generally considered a luxury.

Pheasant are sold in a brace of a cock and hen bird – the latter being the smaller, though more tender. I always like to keep a few of the cock feathers, which really are rather beautiful, to garnish the finished dish as they did in Victorian times.

---

1 brace pheasant, plucked, drawn and trussed
8 rashers streaky bacon
8 crushed juniper berries
water   ½ tsp dried thyme

Place the pheasant in a roasting tin, into which you have poured a little water, about ½ inch in depth. Scatter the juniper berries and thyme in the water. Cover the breasts and legs with bacon and cover the whole tin with foil, sealing the edges. Cook at gas mark 5, 375°F, 190°C, for 45 minutes to an hour, removing the foil for the last ten minutes. Lift the pheasant onto a warmed serving dish and keep hot.

Boil the cooking liquids in the tin until reduced to a third, scraping up the residue. Serve with game chips.

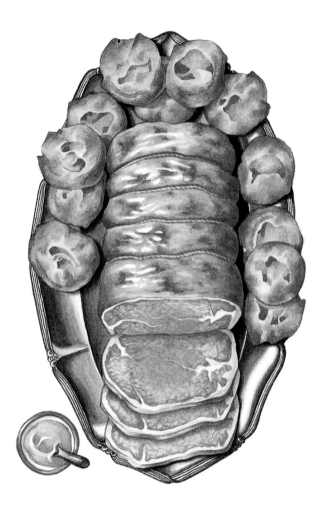

Roast Beef

The traditional Sunday roast, a time for all the family to get together and enjoy good food and conversation.

Take 6-7 lb / 3 kg sirloin of beef on the bone, rub a little salt over it and place in a preheated oven at gas mark 8, 450°F, 220°C for 25 minutes, then reduce the heat to gas mark 4, 350°F, 180°C. Cook for a further hour, by which time you will have well done beef on the outside and medium on the inside. Reduce or increase the times indicated depending on your individual taste.

Yorkshire Puddings
8 oz / 250 g / 2¼ cups plain flour
½ pt / 300 ml / 1¼ cups milk
a little salt
1 tsp oil
2 eggs

Combine all the above ingredients in a mixing bowl and using an electric whisk, whisk until mixed to a smooth batter. Let stand for one hour.

Spoon two tablespoons of fat off the roast beef and put a little into each hole of a 12-hole bun tin. Divide the batter between the bun tins (do not overfill), and put in the oven, once you have cooked the beef and raised the heat again to gas mark 6, 425°F, 200°C. Cook the yorkshires for about 15 minutes or until well risen and golden brown.

The roast beef would traditionally be served with a brown gravy, horseradish sauce and accompanied by a selection of fresh seasonal vegetables and roast potatoes.

Salmon with Dill Butter

There has always been much argument between the various regions of the country as to whose salmon is the best. To my mind it is equally as good provided it is served really fresh. Fresh herbs are of course preferable, but dried dill may be used equally successfully in this recipe.

---

4 salmon steaks	2 tsp lemon juice
3 oz/75 g/6 tbsp butter, melted	freshly ground black pepper
1 tbsp finely chopped fresh dill	4 slices of lemon

Preheat the grill (broiler) to medium. Brush the salmon all over with a little of the melted butter and season with black pepper. Grill the salmon, for about 3-4 minutes each side, until the flesh comes away from the bone when a sharp knife is inserted – do not overcook. Meanwhile, over a gentle heat, reheat the melted butter and stir in the dill and lemon juice.

Remove the salmon onto a serving dish. Pour over the dill butter and garnish with twists of lemon.

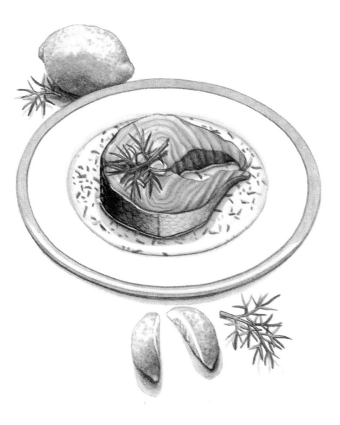

Crown Roast of Lamb

Spring lamb reared on the salty grasslands of Romney Marsh in the south-east of England is the most delicious. Crown Roast is a traditional, if flamboyant, way of serving lamb at Easter.

2 best ends of lamb (12-14 cutlets), trimmed	1 oz/25 g/2 tbsp sultanas
1 small onion	3 medium cooking apples
1 stick celery	6 oz/150 g cooked long grain rice
3 tbsp sunflower oil	1½ tbsp finely chopped fresh parsley
grated rind and juice of ½ lemon	8 fl oz/240 ml/1 cup cider (or apple juice)
3 carrots	

Bend the lamb around to form a crown and secure with skewers and string. Twist foil around the exposed bone-ends and stand the crown in a roasting tin.

Peel and finely chop the onion, carrots and celery. Peel, core and finely dice the apples. Heat the oil in a frying pan and cook the onion and celery until the onion is soft and transparent. Add the carrots, sultanas and apples and continue cooking. Mix in the rice, lemon rind, juice and parsley. Season with salt and pepper. Press the mixture into the centre of the crown, and then brush the meat and stuffing with a little oil.

Roast at gas mark 4, 375°F, 180°C for 1½ to 2 hours. Remove meat from roasting tin, and pour off any fat, leaving the juices. Add the cider to the tin and cook gently, stirring with a wooden spoon. Season and boil up into gravy and serve separately.

Mackerel · Gooseberry Sauce

Mackerel is an inexpensive fish caught in abundance around the shores of the West Country. It's an oily fish which the sharpness of the gooseberry offsets perfectly.

4 medium sized mackerel, gutted	a little cider
1 lemon	8 oz/250 g gooseberries, topped and tailed
freshly ground black pepper	1 oz/25 g/2 tbsp butter
	2 oz/50 g/4 tbsp sugar

Place the fish in a shallow ovenproof dish. Thinly slice the lemon and place on top of the mackerel. Season with a little pepper, and pour over a little cider, just to moisten the bottom of the dish. Cover with foil and seal well. Bake for 25 minutes at gas mark 5, 375°F, 190°C.

Meanwhile cook the gooseberries with the sugar and 3 tablespoons of water until soft. Transfer the fruit to a food processor or liquidizer and process until smooth. Pass through a sieve to remove the pips and then beat in the butter.

Remove the mackerel from the oven. Arrange on a warmed serving dish, pour over the gooseberry sauce and garnish with a twist of lemon and a sprig of parsley.

Buckinghamshire Clanger

This dish reminds me so much of my childhood, during and just after the war when food was rationed and feeding a family was no easy job. My mother was then, and is still now at 85, a good plain cook, and this was one of her economical, but nourishing, and warming, winter meals for our family. It was what we would call good 'rib-sticking' food, especially on a cold and wet winter day when it was a delight to come home from school to find this set before us.

8 oz/250 g/2¼ cups self-raising flour	water to mix
3 oz/75 g/6 tbsp shredded suet	8 rashers streaky bacon
pinch of salt	1 large onion
	2 medium potatoes

Mix the flour, suet and salt together, and mix into a firm dough with the water. Roll out the pastry on a well floured board into a rectangle about 12 inches (30 cm) square (the pastry should be quite thick).

Remove the rind from the bacon and chop quite finely. Peel and finely chop the onion. Peel and coarsely grate the potatoes. Mix the bacon, onion and potato together, season with salt and pepper and spread evenly over the pastry, leaving about a 1½ inch border all the way round.

Very carefully roll the pastry up like a swiss roll, seal the

28

edge well with water, then fold over the two ends and seal well. Using a double thickness of greaseproof paper (the inner one should be lightly greased) wrap the 'clanger' neatly. Then wrap in foil and seal well. Steam for 1½-2 hours. Serve with fresh seasonal vegetables.

Lancashire Hot~Pot

One of my husband's favourite winter dishes from his native North-West. It is just the dish to serve on a cold winter day.

1½ lbs/675 g lamb chops
2 lamb's kidneys
1 large onion
6 large potatoes
1 tsp curry powder
salt and pepper
¾ pt/350 ml/1¾ cups stock

Skin, core and thickly slice the kidneys. Peel and slice the onion and potatoes. Using a large casserole dish arrange the chops, kidneys and onions in layers. Season with salt and pepper, sprinkle with the curry powder, and cover with the stock. Arrange the potato slices, slightly overlapping on top. Cover the casserole and bake for 2 hours at gas mark 4, 350°F, 180°C, removing the lid for the last 30 minutes to brown the potatoes.

Steak and Kidney Pudding

Mrs Beeton in her *Book of Household Management,* 1861, advises that this traditional pie be sent to the table in its basin, either in an ornamental dish or with a linen napkin pinned round it.

8 oz/250 g/2¼ cups self-raising flour	1½ lbs/675 g lean beef steak
4 oz/100 g/½ cup shredded suet	3 tbsp plain flour
salt and freshly ground black pepper	¼ pt/150 ml/5/8 cup good beef stock
2 lamb's kidneys	¼ pt/150 ml/5/8 cup red wine

Put the suet and flour into a mixing bowl, season with salt and pepper and mix with sufficient water to form a firm dough. Roll out two-thirds of the pastry and use it to line a greased two-pint basin. Cut the meat into small cubes and thinly slice the kidneys, tossing them in seasoned flour. Arrange the meat and kidney in layers in the basin. Mix the stock and wine together and pour over the meat to three-quarters of the way up the basin.

Roll out the remaining pastry to form a lid, sealing well round the edges with water. Cover with a double thickness of greaseproof paper, pleated in the middle, and secure with string. Lower into boiling water and cook for four hours, topping up with hot water as necessary, to ensure the saucepan does not boil dry.

Bubble and Squeak

This dish again demonstrates the thriftiness of the English housewife. A typical Monday vegetable dish, an excellent way of using up left-over potato and 'greens', and delicious served with grilled sausages and bacon.

---

left-over mashed potatoes
left-over cooked cabbage
salt and freshly ground black pepper
1 oz/25 g/2 tbsp butter

Mix the potato and cabbage together in a large mixing bowl, and season with salt and black pepper. Melt the butter in a heavy bottomed frying pan and add the vegetable mixture, pressing it down firmly with a palette knife. Cook until nicely browned underneath, turn over, and brown the underside.

Other cooked vegetables such as carrots, parsnips, turnip, peas, leeks etc., can also be added.

Cornish Pasties

Pastry rolled out like a plate
Piled with turmut, tates and mate,
Doubled up and baked like fate
That's a Cornish pasty.

The pasty was devised as an easy means for the

farmworkers and miners of Cornwall to convey their midday meal to work.

1 lb/450 g/4½ cups self-raising flour	1 large potato
3 oz/75 g/4 tbsp margarine	1 medium turnip
½ tsp salt	1 medium onion
8 oz/250 g beef skirt, trimmed	salt and freshly ground black pepper
	water

Sift the flour and salt into a mixing bowl, rub the fat into the flour until the mixture resembles coarse breadcrumbs and mix in water to make a pliable dough. Roll out the pastry and cut into 6 x 8 inch (20 cm) rounds.

Finely dice the meat, peel and dice the turnip and potato. Peel and finely chop the onion. Mix all the filling ingredients together, season with salt and pepper, and divide between the pastry rounds.

Dampen the edges with water and draw the pastry over the filling, sealing the edges well. With thumb and forefinger 'crimp' the sealed edges, folding over to form a double seal. Brush with a little beaten egg, place on a baking sheet and cook for 15 minutes at gas mark 8, 450°F, 220°C. Reduce the heat and cook for a further 45 minutes at gas mark 4, 350°F, 180°C.

Baked Stuffed Potatoes

I can remember, as a girl, sitting a domestic science examination, and one of the dishes I had to prepare was this one. I don't think I can improve on it after so many years practice!

4 even sized large potatoes	1 tsp finely chopped onion
4 oz/100 g/½ cup grated Cheddar cheese	1 oz/25 g/2 tbsp butter
2 firm ripe tomatoes, sliced	a little milk
	sea salt

Scrub the potatoes well, dry and prick all over with a fork, then rub a little sea salt into the skins (this will make them lovely and crisp). Bake near the top of the oven at gas mark 6, 400°F, 200°C for about an hour. Remove from the oven and use a clean tea towel to handle the potatoes. Cut them in half lengthwise. Using a teaspoon, carefully scoop out the potato into a bowl, leaving the skin intact like a shell.

Mash the potato lightly then mix in the cheese (reserving about a tablespoon), the onion, butter and a little milk, season with salt and freshly ground black pepper, mix really well, then spoon the mixture back into the potato cases. Top each half potato with a little grated cheese and a slice of tomato. Pop under the grill and cook until the cheese has melted and is golden and bubbling.

Cauliflower Cheese

Cauliflower has been one of our most popular vegetables since the sixteenth century when it was first introduced from the East. I find that dividing the cauliflower into florettes before cooking produces a more evenly cooked result.

1 large cauliflower	1 tsp Dijon mustard
1 1/2 oz/40 g/3 tbsp butter	salt and white pepper
1 tbsp flour	2 tbsp fresh breadcrumbs
1/2 pt/300 ml/1 1/4 cups milk	1 tbsp grated Cheddar cheese
3 oz/75 g/6 tbsp grated Cheddar cheese	1 tbsp grated Parmesan cheese

Trim the cauliflower, carefully break into florettes and cook in lightly salted boiling water until just tender. Drain well and transfer to a shallow ovenproof dish.

Melt the butter in a saucepan and stir in the flour, mixing well, and cook for 2 minutes. Over a medium heat gradually stir in the milk, bring to the boil, lower the heat and simmer until the mixture thickens and is smooth. Stir in the mustard and 3 oz grated Cheddar cheese, remove from the heat and season with salt and pepper. Pour the sauce over the cauliflower.

Mix the breadcrumbs and remaining grated cheeses together and sprinkle evenly over the cauliflower. Bake in the oven for 15 minutes at gas mark 6, 400°F, 200°C until the topping is golden brown.

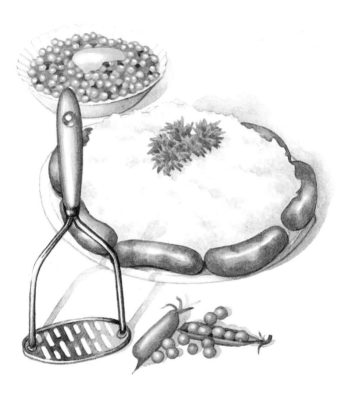

Sausages 'n' Mash

One of England's favourite foods, popular with all ages. The English eat well over a hundred sausages per head per year, which proves their popularity beyond doubt. They vary in flavour, colour, size and seasoning from region to region, but pork sausages are the ones most generally eaten.

---

6 large potatoes
1 oz/25 g/2 tbsp butter
a little milk
salt and pepper
1 lb/450 g pork sausages

Peel and roughly cut up the potatoes and cook them with a little salt in boiling water until tender. Drain well and then mash, mixing in the butter, a little milk, and salt and pepper.

Arrange the sausages on a grill pan and cook, without the addition of any fats of any kind, under a medium heat, turning frequently until golden brown.

Arrange the sausages and mashed potatoes on a warm serving dish. You can garnish with some fried onion rings, cooked until golden brown, and brown gravy may be served separately.

Summer Pudding

A truly wonderful dessert, which I make when the soft fruits in my garden are profuse. Any soft fruit can be used but I particularly like the combination of raspberries, blackcurrants and gooseberries.

1½ lbs/675 g/4-5 cups mixed soft fruits
8 oz/250 g/1 cup granulated sugar
8 slices white bread

Pick over the fruit, removing any stalks, wash if necessary then cook with the water and sugar until just soft. Cut the crusts off the bread and arrange the slices in a 1½ pint pudding basin (retain a couple of slices for the top). Pour the fruit and juices, while still warm, into the basin. Use the remaining bread to top the pudding, trimming to fit. Put a saucer on top of the pudding, and weigh down with a large tin on top. Refrigerate overnight.

To serve loosen round the edges with a palette knife, turn out onto a serving dish and decorate with whipped cream and more fresh fruit. Incidentally, this dish freezes exceptionally well.

Sherry Trifle

Trifles became very popular in Victorian times, when they were often presented as the centrepiece dessert, piled high with custard or whipped cream and lavishly decorated with almonds, cherries, crystallised fruits and flowers.

8 trifle sponges	1 pt/600 ml/2½ cups milk
6 tbsp raspberry or strawberry jam	2 oz/50 g/4 tbsp caster sugar
¼ pt/150ml/5/8 cup sherry	½ pt/300 ml/1 cup double cream
6 oz/150 g macaroons	glacé cherries, angelica, almonds
4 egg yolks	

Cut the trifle sponges in half and spread with jam, sandwich together and cut into cubes. Arrange in the bottom of a glass dish. Break up the macaroons and spread over the top. Pour over the sherry, cover with cling film and let stand for an hour or so.

Meanwhile put the milk into a saucepan and bring gently to just below boiling point. Beat the egg yolks with the sugar, and pour over the hot milk, whisking all the time. Transfer the custard to a clean pan and cook very gently, over a low heat, stirring all the time until the custard thickens. Remove from heat and allow to cool a little before pouring over the trifle. Return the dish to the refrigerator, and allow to set overnight.

Whip the cream until thick but not stiff, and pile on top of the custard. Decorate with the cherries, squares of angelica and almonds.

Traditional Christmas Turkey

Roast turkey with chestnut stuffing, bacon rolls and chipolata sausages is traditionally eaten on Christmas Day, accompanied by roast potatoes, and a selection of winter vegetables: brussels sprouts, parsnips, carrots and leeks. Bread sauce should be served separately as should a boat of gravy.

As turkeys can dry out during the roasting process I have found that a piece of butter muslin soaked in melted butter and draped over the breast of the bird keeps it quite moist during cooking.

Chestnut and Sausage Stuffing
(sufficient for a 13 lb/6 kg turkey)
1 lb/450 g sausage meat
1 lb/450 g chestnuts
salt and freshly ground black pepper

Place sausagemeat in a bowl and season well with salt and pepper. Make a cut around the sides of the chestnuts and place in boiling water for 5 minutes. Peel while still warm, then mince in a food processor. Mix in with the sausagemeat and use to stuff the turkey.

Salt and pepper the turkey, place on a rack in the oven

and cook at gas mark 4, 350°F, 180°C for about 2½ hours, or until a skewer, inserted into the thickest part of the leg, comes out cleanly and the juices run clear.

Chipolata sausages and bacon rolls can be cooked during the last half hour of cooking time.

Christmas Pudding

This recipe was given to me by a very good friend who is a keen cook. It is absolutely delicious and has been passed down from generation to generation of his family.

1 lb/450 g/2 cups shredded suet	8 oz/250 g/2 cups mixed peel
8 oz/250 g/2¼ cups self-raising flour	small tin crushed pineapple, drained
8 oz/250 g/2¼ cups fresh breadcrumbs	4 eggs, beaten
1 lb/450 g/2⅔ cups raisins	1 tsp baking powder
1 lb/450 g/2⅔ cups currants	4 oz/100 g/½ cup soft brown sugar
1 lb/450 g/2⅔ cups sultanas	½ tsp ground nutmeg
rind and juice of a lemon	1 lb/450 g/1½ cups golden syrup, warmed
	2-3 tbsp rum or whisky
	a little milk

Combine all the dry ingredients in a large mixing bowl, stir in the crushed pineapple, beaten eggs, rind and juice of a lemon and mix well. Add syrup and whisky (or rum) and mix thoroughly – this is the time to stir in some little silver coins or silver charms if you wish – then add a little milk and mix again. Put into prepared basins, seal with a double thickness of foil and boil for six hours.

An English Cheeseboard

Cheese has always been popular with the English, particularly as an alternative to dessert, when it is best served accompanied by some home-grown local apples. There is a great variety of English cheeses, ranging from Cheshire, the oldest of English cheeses, known in Roman Britain and a favourite of Queen Elizabeth I, to the new cheeses of today like Huntsman, an unusual combination of Double Gloucester and Stilton, and Yarg, a distinctive nettle-wrapped Cornish cheese. When preparing a cheeseboard it is important to have a variation of flavour, from mild to strong. A typical English cheeseboard should consist of some of the following:

Cheddar Since the sixteenth century Cheddar has traditionally been made in the Mendip Hills, close to the Cheddar Gorge in Somerset.

Leicester A rich deep orange cheese, with a mellow flavour.

Blue Stilton Known as the 'King of English Cheeses', creamy coloured with blue veins and a rough natural crust.

Nutwood A delicious blend of Cheddar, hazlenuts, raisins and cider.

Lymeswold The first soft blue cheese to be produced in England.

Cheeses should be taken out of the refrigerator about 2 hours before you need them, and arranged on a cheeseboard. Accompany them with some crisp water biscuits, sticks of fresh celery, trimmed and put into a small jug of water, and a bowl of really seasonal fruits, all in readiness for the great English cheese treat.

Mulled Wine

Traditionally served around Christmas time, mulled wine is delicious and warming on a cold winter evening. I like to have a big pan of it, steaming gently, ready for when the carol singers call on Christmas Eve. Accompanied by hot mince pies it chases away all the winter chills.

2 pts/1 litre/5 cups robust red table wine	1 tsp ground nutmeg
½ bottle port	2 oz/50 g/½ cup brown sugar
¼ pt/150 ml/5/8 cup brandy	1 lemon 8 cloves
	2 tsp ground cinnamon

Stick the cloves into the lemon and put with other ingredients in a large saucepan. Heat slowly, stirring often, until as hot as possible without boiling. Taste and add more sugar if required. Ladle into warmed mugs or punch glasses.

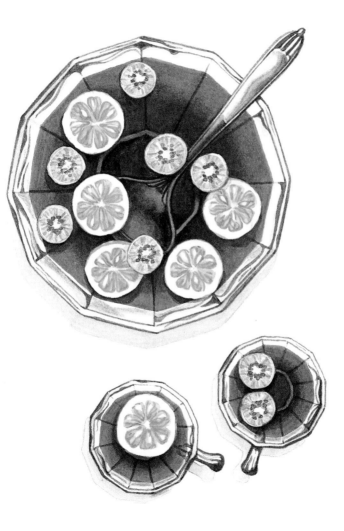

Index